Good Ole Boys

by
William M. Ross II

authorHOUSE®

AuthorHouse™
1663 Liberty Drive
Bloomington, IN 47403
www.authorhouse.com
Phone: 833-262-8899

Published by AuthorHouse 12/09/2020

ISBN: 978-1-4343-3693-4(sc)
ISBN: 978-1-4343-3694-1 (hc)

Library of Congress Control Number: 2007907055

Print information available on the last page.

Any people depicted in stock imagery provided by Getty Images are models,
and such images are being used for illustrative purposes only.
Certain stock imagery © Getty Images.

This book is printed on acid-free paper.

Dedication

This book is dedicated to the memory of my mother and father, who taught me that there are far greater riches in this world than those that can be deposited in a bank account!

Author's Note

To prevent confusion on the reader's part, it is necessary to note that I was named after my father. Therefore, there are two Bills in these stories. Until I was about twelve years old, our neighbors, and everyone else, referred to us as "Little Bill" and "Big Bill." After that, until my dad died, it was "Young Bill" and "Old Bill."

About two years ago, I was advised that the third member of my old group of friends had died. This news motivated me to write this little book for my children, grandchildren, and generations unborn. I hope that they may laugh at the amusing stories, and learn from those that are not. I wanted to share these stories, because I am the last of the four "good ole boys!"

Bill Ross
Pineville, Missouri
June, 2007

In Appreciation

I wish to express my deepest gratitude to my neighbor of more than twenty five years! Jo Pearcy is a wonderful, warm lady, without whose help, I could not have written this book! Jo is an author of marvelous children's books! Her expert help, advice, and kindly encouragement have enabled me to write this little book! Jo also created the original artwork for the cover.

Thanks Jo!

Forward

In these days of huge corporate farms, huge machines, with air conditioned operator cabs, two-way radios, GPS systems, and computerized efficiency, there is hardly a remnant of the type and size farm on which I grew to a man. Although, there are some exceptions, the "farmer" of today is not really a farmer. He is a planter. He concentrates on one or two crops that he sells for cash when harvested.

This book is about a way of living, that embodied a cycle of life which reflected values not often seen today. The cycle of birth, growth, maturity, death, and rebirth was repeated over and over again. The "family" farm was just that. Generally, two, and sometimes three generations were involved. Each family member did a share of the work.

This was also a time in which farming was in a state of change. This was caused largely due to the loss of manpower during WWII. During this time, horsepower and human labor were gradually replaced by machines. The introduction of electricity to rural America was also a major factor in the modernization process.

My dad was an average farmer of that time and in that area. We had a dairy, plus beef cattle, horses, hogs, and at one time, a few sheep. My mother had a large flock of chickens, some geese, and turkeys. (All various fowl were considered property of the wife, and she received the income from them to buy things for the household) The crops were wheat, corn, milo, soy beans, barley, and oats. Hay was harvested for winter feed. Some crops were sold for cash. This mostly being wheat and milo in our area. Most of the other crops were stored on the farm to provide feed for the livestock. We had a very large garden, which was also my mother's domain.

In retrospect, I guess it was a hard life. My dad's day began before dawn and ended after dark. My mother's day was only slightly shorter. This was every day except Sunday. On Sunday, we did only the daily chores required to care for the animals. Sunday was for church, rest, and visits with aunts, uncles, and friends. In spite of the long hours of work, it was a good life. The close ties between parents and children instilled the value of hard work, thrift, and honesty.

The stories in this book are not in chronological order. The events are real! I have related them just as they happened. Some of the names have been changed to protect the guilty, as well as the innocent. Conversations, at which I was present are written as accurately as an old man can remember them. I have taken some literary license with conversations at which I was not present. This was necessary to set the background for events which did happen! The time frame for this book is the early nineteen forties, through the nineteen fifties. The lifestyle described above is the background for this book about the life of a Kansas farm boy. One of the "**Good Ole Boys.**"

Contents

Dedication   v

Author's Note   vi

In Appreciation   vii

Forward   ix

Chapter 1
Corn Cobs   1

Chapter 2
Runaway   5

Chapter 3
Is Honor Sacred ?   9

Chapter 4
Haying Time   13

Chapter 5
Junior Farmers   17

Chapter 6
School Days   23

Chapter 7
The Tax Man Cometh   29

Chapter 8
Farm Dogs   35

Chapter 9
Country Doctors   39

Chapter 10
A Dollars Worth   45

Chapter 11
Guests   51

Chapter 12
    Hunting Elusive Snipe   59

Chapter 13
    Outhouses   63

Chapter 14
    Farm Women   71

Chapter 15
    Home Brew   79

Chapter 16
    Rustlers!   83

Chapter 17
    Killers   89

Chapter 18
    Pie Suppers   99

Chapter 19
    Bedtime   103

Chapter 20
    Ice Skating   107

Chapter 21
    Beauty   111

Chapter 1
Corn Cobs

Billboy come here ! Now, Billboy isn't my name. My mom always called me Billy. My dad usually called me son. except when he was disgusted or angry with me or required an instant response. So a "Billboy" summons was not to be ignored! As a matter of fact, it was to be obeyed instantly! I climbed down from the barn loft, where I and my pal, Jim, had been catching pigeons.

It was the summer of 1948, just before my tenth birthday. In those days, there being no television, indeed no electricity on our farm, kids had to provide their own entertainment. On this particular day, Jim and I had decided to have some entertainment with corn cobs that was now probably going to put the seat of our pants in jeopardy!

In those days corn cobs had many uses on the farm. They were ground and used for livestock bedding, chicken litter, insulation, or used whole as toilet paper, (we didn't use them for this. We used mail order catalogs.) as well as fire starters in the wood stove in winter time. The list of useful items goes on and on. However, Jim and I had put a corn cob to another use!

When I got outside the barn, I took off at a run toward the sound of Dad's voice with ole Jim trailing a few paces behind. Dad's voice had come from the chicken pen about 150 yards away, so that is where I headed for.

Sure enough, I found Dad standing in the chicken pen.

The pen was about 75 feet square, enclosed by a wire mesh about eight feet high. The pen was attached to the chicken house where the chickens roosted at night. The chickens were kept inside of this pen to protect them from coons, skunks, coyotes and other predators who liked chicken dinner.

When Jim and I arrived at a dead run, Dad, with a stern look on his face, looked me in the eye and said "What about this?"

Now, I could be pretty obtuse when it was required, so I answered "About what?"

However, this wasn't going to work, as a blind man could see what "what" was! There were about 100 hens in the pen and one large rooster. About a dozen of the hens were squatting on the ground with their wings spread out and making clucking sounds that they usually made when they were sitting on a nest of hatching eggs!

On that day Mom was doing laundry up at the house, and Dad was out in the hay field. Thus Jim and I had been left to our ourselves! This wasn't unusual. Farm parents in those days were too busy with the hard work of survival to constantly watch what a pair of nine year old boys were doing!

In the middle of the afternoon Mom had heard the rooster crowing his fool head off about every 60 seconds! She had come out to the chicken pen to see why he was doing it, as he usually only crowed early in the morning.

The rooster was running from one squatting hen to another. He would mount a hen, and try to have sex with her, which was impossible, because the hen was hunkered down in the dirt. He would jump off, flap his wings, crow like he had accomplished something, and then run and mount the next one and repeat the process!

When Dad came in from the hay field, Mom told him "There is something wrong with my hens, and I think that rooster has gone crazy! I don't know what is wrong with him!" Dad went to the chicken pen. He took one look. "I know what's wrong! Billboy, come here!" Then he told Mom to go to the house and get some lard.

Back to Dad and I; "You know what! Where's th' cob?"

"I just wanted to see what would happen."

"Now you know! Grab that crazy rooster!"

Well, to make the story short, Jim and I caught the rooster and each one of the hens. Dad turned them up and rubbed lard on each ones butt, and their behavior returned to normal.

Although, I had anticipated the worst, when it was all over, Dad looked at us with a small grin, and said "don't you boys ever do this again."

I think this was because he knew that a couple of weeks before, I had overheard him telling my uncle Charlie how, when he was a kid, he had put turpentine on a corncob, and rubbed a roosters butt with it!

Chapter 2
Runaway

"Whoa Senator, whoa Maud !" My dad stood like a rock directly in front of more than 2 ton of horseflesh bearing down on him at a dead run! Again, he threw his arms up high and yelled in his big voice, "whoa Senator, whoa Maud"! The big horses were used to obeying him, and they obeyed this time, coming to a halt in front of him. Dad walked around to the wagon load of corn stalk bundles and lifted me off the wagon where I was clinging for dear life.

It was the year 1944, just before my 6th birthday. I had been feeling really proud of myself. During those war years, manpower was hard to find. My dad was putting corn silage in the big upright grey silos. These structures were large round vertical tubes, made of concrete. They were about 30 ft. in diameter and about 8 stories tall. The livestock feed that was stored in them was called silage.

In those days, the process of making silage entailed gathering green corn stalks that had been cut and bundled, and loading them on bundle wagons for the ½ mile trip from the corn field to the silos. Upon arrival there, the bundles were fed into a silage chopper, and blown up a pipe into the silo. During the war years gasoline was in short supply, so the wagons were being pulled by teams of horses. These were Percheron horses. Each huge animal weighed over a ton. However, they were very gentle, and obeyed voice commands.

When the work crew was assembled, Dad found that he was short one man. After being unable to find another man, he decided that I could drive the teams back and forth to the field. I had driven both teams many times and knew all the voice commands which they would obey. These were "gee, haw, back, and whoa".

All went well for the first two days. Dad would lift me onto an empty wagon. I would pick up the lines, (these were leather straps about ¾ inch wide X 15 feet long) and drive the team and wagon to the field. There, my 16 year old brother, Merle would lift me off the empty wagon and put me on a full one. I would then drive the loaded wagon back to the silo. By switching two teams between three wagons, the chopper was able to run continuously .

"I told you not to run those horses Billboy!"

As I broke into tears, I replied "I didn't do it on purpose Dad. When the wagon rolled down that little hump at the end of the field, and the harness bretchen hit their rear ends, they started to run and I couldn't stop them!"

Now, the bretchen is a wide heavy belt that goes around the hips of the horse. It's function is to allow the horse to push in reverse any load such as a wagon. Dad looked down at me, and walked to the horse's rear. He ran his hand between the bretchen and the horse. His hand came away with a bunch of cockleburs. He got a grim look on his face. "It's O.K. son." To the two men helping at the silo, "I'm taking this wagon back to the field with Bill."

When we got to the field, he got off the wagon and unsnapped one of the lines. He went up to Merle with the cockleburs in one hand, and the folded lines in the other. He said to Merle;

"How did these burrs get under the horse harness?"

"I was just having a little fun!"

"Do you realize that your little brother could have been killed? Let's see if you think its funny five minutes from now. Come around here with me!" They were gone around the far side of the loaded wagon about five minutes. When they returned, Dad put the line back on the harness, and we went back to the house.

I hauled bundles for 4 days, and earned my first dollar in wages. It was an enormous sum of money to a 6 year old boy!

Merle ate supper that night standing up!

Chapter 3

Is Honor Sacred ?

When the founders of our country signed the declaration of independence, they pledged their lives, their fortunes, and their **sacred** honor. Sadly, it is now thought by many people to be a quaint phrase, no longer applicable in the modern world of the 21st. Century. I can remember a time when men valued their word as a badge of honor. My dad was one of those men. My dad had no bad vices that I ever knew of ! His word, once given could be etched in stone! His neighbors were men cast in the same mold. The old farmers of his generation did most of their business with each other on a handshake.

My dad taught (or tried to teach) me many things about honor, morality, decency and honesty. The following little story illustrates the type of men who were truly "the salt of the earth".

One night in late fall, after Dad and I had finished doing chores, and were on our way to the house, we noticed a red glow in the sky about a mile east of us. We came to the quick conclusion that it was a house or barn on fire! We jumped in the pickup truck and took off in that direction to see if we could be of any help. When we arrived at the scene, we discovered that it was our neighbor, Elton Ewell's big cattle and hay barn. By this time, the barn was totally engulfed in flames and there was nothing anyone could do.

Two days after the fire, Elton came to see my dad. They sat at the kitchen table and he explained his problem. I sat and listened and kept my mouth shut. In those days kids were to be seen and not heard. Elton told Dad that his entire winter supply of hay had been destroyed in the barn fire. Now, we had an excess of hay that year. Our barn was full, plus we had about 2,000 bales stacked outside. The conversation went like this.

"Bill, I haven't got any hay left for feed this winter. If you've got any extra, I would like to buy it. But I haven't got any extra cash right now."

"Well, I've got plenty of hay. You can go out to the stack in the feed lot and get what you need."

They then agreed that Elton would pay ten cents a bale at harvest time, or replace the hay from his next hay crop. As the winter wore on, Elton would come over from time to time and haul off a load of hay.

At this time, I was a freshman in high school. One of my classes was economics. My dad had only gone through the eighth grade, so I decided to demonstrate my superior financial knowledge to him. One evening I proceeded to enlighten him about contracts, debts, profit, etc. etc.

"Dad, Elton has hauled a lot of hay out of that big stack in the feed lot."

Dad got a very sober look on his face. "Yes he has. It's a good thing we had enough extra to take care of him this winter."

"Well do you know how much he has taken?"

"Not exactly, but he knows"

"Shouldn't you have been counting it?"

"Why should I? He knows how to count."

I was getting exasperated!

"You should have a written contract stating the terms of the agreement! You also should have had his signature, agreeing to the terms!"

Dad was getting a little exasperated himself!

"Billboy, let me explain something to you that you're not going to find in your school books! It's a thing called honor! Elton is my neighbor! I know him to be an honorable man! Being an honorable man, he is also honest! How does he know that I won't raise the price when it comes time to settle up? He knows because I am also an honorable man! If you can't trust a man's word, don't do business with him, because his signature is no better than his word."

Elton was an honorable man. At the next hay season, he replaced all the borrowed hay! Dad hadn't counted the hay when it had been taken. Neither did he count it when it was returned!

Chapter 4
Haying Time

Cutting and harvesting hay for the livestock in those days was a community enterprise. It involved putting together a work force of neighboring farmers. Generally this involved a farmer and one or two of his teenage sons from surrounding farms. It worked like this.

A hay baler was an expensive piece of equipment. Not all farmers had hay balers. When haying time came around neighbors would get together and form a hay "crew". This crew would then go from farm to farm, mowing, raking and baling each farmers hay in succession. Each farmer would contribute various tractors, mowers, rakes, wagons, etc. plus labor. The farm where the baling was taking place, would furnish tractor fuel, and baling wire.

The farmers wife was expected to prepare the noon meal for the entire crew. This was a hard task, as the crew usually consisted of ten to twelve men and boys. The work was strenuous, and the hours long for the crew, and they expected to eat well! One of my most pleasant memories is of my mom's meals during hay season. The menu consisted of golden fried chicken that Mom had killed at about 6:00 that morning. Plus mashed potatoes, gravy, fresh green beans from the garden, fresh peas and carrots, fresh baked home made hot rolls, followed by apple pie, all washed down with gallons of iced tea.

Each evening, all the men and boys would get a bar of soap, a towel, and clean clothes that they had brought with them in the morning. Then everyone would get in one of the farm trucks and head for a farm pond. Several of the farms had ponds that were fed by clear springs. They made excellent bathing pools. Upon arriving at the pond, everyone would shuck off all their clothes and jump in.

Therein lies the story of how Crawdad Russell got his name! That summer, Elmo (his given name) and I were almost 16 years old. However, he was a year behind me in school. Ole Elmo was as strong as a bull, but he wasn't exactly the brightest bulb in the lamp. He was also well endowed in the male organ department. He was always bragging about this part of his anatomy.

On this particular evening, there was a lot of horseplay, as there always was when you got a pack of teenage farm boys together. An other interesting thing about Elmo was that he was the only one that couldn't swim! While the rest of us jumped, dived, and wrestled in the deep water, Elmo always stayed in the shallow water. Suddenly someone looked across the pond and saw that Elmo had paddled about 50 yards into the shallow end of the pond and was lying on his belly in less than a foot of water! This shallow part of the pond had a mud bottom, unlike where we were, which had a gravel bottom.

"Elmo, get out of there!" Too late!

"**Yeowooo!**" Ole Elmo came straight up out of the water!

They look like small lobsters. City folks call them crayfish. Country boys call them crawdads. Another name for them is mudbug! This is because they like to hide in holes on mud bottoms and wait for something to eat pass by. When Elmo came by, I guess he dragged something past one of their hideouts that looked like a tasty morsel!

Well, sure enough! When ole Elmo stood up, there dangling from the end of his pride and joy was--- you guessed it! None of the farm boys I knew were circumcised. But I'm not too sure about Crawdad, because when Jim yanked the crawdad off him, he didn't bother to unclamp the claws!

Chapter 5
Junior Farmers

It was the practice on most farms, that when a boy reached an age his dad deemed proper, he was allowed to farm some land of his own and to own livestock. Late in the winter of 1951, Dad called me to the kitchen table to have a serious talk. This was where most serious talks took place. The talk wasn't about the birds and the bees. A farm boy, 12 years old, already had a working knowledge about reproduction! He began the conversation with, "Well, you've proven that you're big enough to do a man's work. So I guess you're big enough to have some land of your own to farm!"

"Great! How much land?"

"Well, for the first year, I think five acres would be about right."

"Swell! Where at?"

"That little calf pasture south of the hay barn is about the right size, and it need's to be plowed up and put in rowcrop. I'll rent that to ya. How does that suit ya?"

"Great! What can I plant?"

"Whatever you like. The decision is your's!"

"Where will I get the seed?"

"I'll loan ya the seed! However, there are some strings attached!"

"Okay, what strings?"

"I will loan you the use of my equipment for free. You will keep track of the fuel and the seed, and pay me for them at harvest time. Also, at harvest time, you will pay me rent of $10.00 per acre. You will do all of the work yourself! I won't help you! You won't work your field on Sunday!"

"That's okay Dad! I can handle it!"

"There's one more thing. I've been giving you a dollar a week spending money, for your field work! I'll continue to do so until your harvest come's in. After harvest, you'll get no more money from me!"

"Will Sis (Sue) still get money after harvest?"

"Yep!"

"Why?"

"She's a girl! You're a boy!" (End of discussion!)

Today's reader may think that Dad was being miserly or harsh. This was not the case. Most farm boys grew up to be farmers. Our fathers were trying to create a sense of responsibility in their sons. They were introducing us to the adult problems that we would face when we were grown. The idea was, that we would learn the rewards for good decisions and the penalty for poor ones! Although, I didn't remain on the farm after I was grown, those early lessons have been beneficial to me all my life!

Well, after agonizing for 2 weeks between corn, milo, and soy beans, I decided on the latter. I sat at the kitchen table for hours on end with a pencil and a "Big Chief" tablet calculating the cost of seed and fuel, the usual harvest date, the yield of grain for each crop, and the market price per bushel that I should be able to expect at a harvest in the future. Each time I asked my dad for advice, he would reply. "You can figure that stuff as well as I can. The decision is yours!"

When I told Dad that I was going to plant soy beans, he merely said "Well, depending on the weather, at harvest, you'll know if you were right!"

That spring I plowed, disced, and harrowed the soil in my little field. When the time was right, I got the seed from Dad and planted my crop. Two days after I had planted the seed, a spring shower came over and put about an inch of water on my field. I went out to my field every evening to see if my beans were sprouting. On about the fourth evening after the rain, full of anxiety, I left the supper table and again went to the field.

The field was covered with neat little rows of soy bean plants! Some were an inch tall, and some were just breaking out of the soil. I began to yell and dance a goofy jig. I made so much noise, that Mom and Dad could hear me in the house! They both came out to see what the racket was about.

"Looks like you've got a good crop." Dad said with a grin.

"Ain't it beautiful?" I said.

"Well, you've got a good start, but remember, it's a long time till harvest. From now on it's in God's hands!"

Dad was right! Although I cultivated the rows of beans every time a few weeds sprouted, the weather was the determining factor. If soy beans get too much rain at the wrong time, they get a blight called rust. If the weather is dry at the wrong time, the bean pods won't fill out. This will severely reduce the yield! God was good to a 12 year old boy that summer! I had a bountiful crop at harvest time which was just after my thirteenth birthday. During the summer, I learned why men like my dad loved farming. I had experienced the jubilation of seeing my hard work cause a brown field to turn green with growing plants! I had endured the anxious days when my crop needed rain, and the ones when there was too much rain! Finally, I had enjoyed the deep sense of satisfaction when the harvest poured from the combine spout into the waiting farm truck!

I had guessed correctly! The market price for soy beans was high, and due to the weather, my harvest was bountiful!

I should have gotten a clue about my decision at the beginning! When I told Dad of my decision, he had also said something else!

"Well, I guess I'll plant around a hundred acres myself."

Chapter 6
School Days

Like many other things during the time period I am writing about; the country school was under-going a transformation.

I graduated from the eighth grade in 1952. Although, by this time, many rural school districts had been combined to form larger schools, ours was not one of them. Our district was the Township we lived in. A Township was (and still is) a political sub-division of the County. It covered an area six by six miles; or thirty-six square miles.

The township was ran by the a three member, elected, Board of Trustees. The school district was ran by a different three member elected board. This board was allocated a budget funded by property taxes. Although, the school board reported to the county school superintendent, it was basically autonomous. The board hired and paid the teacher, and made the decisions on spending school funds.

In those days, men did not run for a position on the school as people do now. (*Yes, I said men! It was a chauvinistic era, when women did not serve on local boards.*) Serving on the board was considered an obligation, and a burden that should be shared by the members of the community. My dad was asked to share this burden twice. The term of office was for 3 years; with one new member being elected every year. As election approached, the sitting school board would approach a man and ask him if he would be willing to serve on the board, to replace the retiring member. If he agreed, his name, and no other person would be placed on the ballot. This was not exactly the democratic process in action, but it worked and kept irresponsible and spendthrift people from handling public funds! (In order to be requested to share the burden of this position, a person had to have a reputation for thrift, in the management of their own affairs.)

At the time I graduated, our district had not yet been combined with any other district. It was pretty much the same as it had been for fifty years. The school house was a white, one room building. Although electricity had reached it in 1949, no other modernization had taken place. Butane gas was available by this time. However, our conservative school board had decided to keep heating with coal. Their reasoning being that coal was cheaper than butane, and there were boys at school, large enough to carry the coal inside from the coal shed.

Maintenance and repairs to school property were also performed at a minimum cost to the school district. For example: If the school house needed new shingles on the roof, the school board would shop for the lowest price for the material. Then, when one of the board members was hauling something to town, he would pick up the material, and haul it back to the school on his return trip.

The repair usually took place in the fall, after field work had been done. It took place on a Saturday, in order not to interfere with school. A general ring on the party lines would announce the date. All adult men and older boys would be requested to come to the school early on the designated date. The wives were requested to bring a covered dish of food, for the noon meal. The men brought tools and ladders with them, and swarmed over the building. As many as thirty men and boys would be working on the building at any time. The result, was that the shingles would be replaced in one day at no labor cost to the school district! The same method was used for everything from painting to mowing the school yard!

Although, the school building was only one room; it was a large room. It measured about 40 X 60 feet. There was room enough for all eight grades, which usually numbered around twenty-five to thirty-five kids.

There was only one teacher for all eight grades. The students sat in rows, with the lower grades in front, and the upper grades in the rear. The teacher's desk sat at the front of the room on a raised platform or stage that ran the entire width of the building. This allowed the teacher to see over the student's heads, and see any mischief going on at the rear of the room. There was a slate "blackboard" on the wall at the rear of the stage. Since all the students faced this wall, the teacher could write lessons that all could see. Everyone could also see you when you were writing such things as "I shall not talk without permission" 100 times on the board!

Sanitation facilities consisted of a sink, which drained outside the building. Sitting by the sink was a white enamel bucket with a dipper in it. Anyone, raising their hand, and being acknowledged, could ask "may I get a drink?" If the answer was yes, the student could leave their seat and get a drink from the dipper. The dipper was then placed back in the bucket for the next person's use. Water from the bucket was also poured into the sink for hand washing. The water bucket was carried in from an outside well, by one of the older boys at the beginning of the day. There were no school lunches. Each student brought his/her lunch from home in a lunch pail that their mothers had packed for them. The meal I liked best was cold fried chicken. The one I disliked the most, was fried egg sandwiches!

Toilets were two wooden structures located at the rear of the school ground, about 100 feet apart. They were labeled "Boys" and "Girls". Each building was about six feet square, with a concrete floor and "stool". Each had a wooden privacy fence on three sides, that prevented anyone from seeing in the door of the little building.

It was this privacy fence that got Elmo in trouble with my older sister, Sue!

Sue was in the eighth grade. Although, she was two years older than me, I was only one grade behind her in school. Elmo was in the sixth grade, although he was only slightly younger than me. He had failed one year of school.

On the day it happened, the weather was rainy and cool. Sue had brought her bumbershoot (umbrella) to school.

During my life, I have noticed certain differences in male and female attitude about toilets. When two or more couples "men and women" are together in a public place such as a restaurant, a man merely excuses himself, and leaves the table when it is necessary to go to the restroom. When a female needs to "powder her nose," she will ask the other one or two women if they want to go along.

This is the way it was at school. The boys would go to the outhouse alone. When the girls went during recess or lunch time, they always went in a flock. I have no profound thoughts on this difference. However, ole Elmo would have been a lot better off if girls didn't have this mysterious (to men) flock impulse. As usual, during lunch hour that day, four girls went to the girls outhouse at the same time. Of the bunch, my sister was the oldest.

Now, Elmo had discovered something about the privacy fence on the little building. There was a knothole in the fence at eye-level! When he saw the girl flock go into the outhouse, he sneaked over, and was peering through the knothole at them. He was, that is, until Sue happened to look directly at that spot in the fence and see an eyeball looking at her. She let out a screech, that would have done justice to a tomcat with his tail caught in a wringer!

The screech gave Elmo a warning that probably saved his eye! He jerked back! As he did so; Sue, being a person of action, jammed the tip of her folded bumbershoot through the hole! It only caught the corner of his eye, and not the eyeball !

Sue, being, as I said, a person of action, launched herself around the fence and began to swat ole Elmo about the head and shoulders! Elmo took off at a run for the school house with Sue on his heels, swatting him with that bumbershoot with both hands. All the while yelling "I'll teach you, you pervert!".

Elmo came to school the next day with the blackest eye you ever saw! Ever after that, when Elmo was hanging around our house, Sue would look at him and mutter "pervert."

I once asked him; " Why don't you say anything back to her?"

"Are you kiddin'? That's the meanest danged gal I ever saw! She'd likely whack me with that danged bumbershoot, or sumpthin' worse!"

Chapter 7
The Tax Man Cometh

RING, RING, RING, RING, RING, Five short rings on the party phone line meant that everyone who heard it was supposed to pick up the receiver. When anyone wanted to alert their neighbors to an emergency, or wanted to make an announcement, this was the preferred method. The announcement on this day was, "The tax man is coming!"

The official name of the person being referred to, was "County Assessor." This elected official had the duty to assess the value of certain property owned by individuals. The state and the county collected tax revenue from the individual based on the worth of their property. There were two types of these taxes. One was known as real estate tax. It was a tax placed on land, and buildings. The other was personal property tax. Everyone hated this tax, as it covered just about everything you owned, except the clothes on your back! This was the reason for the general warning call. This gave people time to hide such things as guns, dogs, silverware, jewelry, etc. etc.

Each year, the farmer would receive a form from the county assessor's office, on which he was supposed to list his personal assets. The assessor would then personally make random visits to different farms, to verify that everything was as listed.

One of the things that was supposed to be listed, was each adult dog owned. They were taxed at the rate of one dollar each. Dad always listed one dog. Most people never listed any! Once, I heard the assessor say to my dad, "We need to elect a county dog catcher!

"Why?"

"Because we are overran with stray dogs."

"Why do you say that?"

"Whenever I see a dog in the yard, I ask, Is that your dog? The answer is always, nope! It's a stray that wandered in here this morning!"

One day, I went over to the Outerbine place, shortly after the general warning went out on the phone. Jim was gone in the pickup. It was noon, and Eddie and his dad were in the kitchen. They invited me to eat with them.

"No thank ya, I just ate. Where's Jim?"

"I sent him to town to get some seed at the elevator."

We were sitting at the table talking, when the assessor drove in the yard. I said "well I guess I'll get along."

"Stick around, Jim ain't goin' to be very long"

Thus, I was still at the table when the assessor, Raymond Dozier, came to the door, and knocked.

"Come in Ray. Have ya eaten?"

"Yeah, my wife packed me a lunch."

After some conversation about the weather and crop prices, Raymond dug some forms out of his briefcase and began listing the Outerbine property. The conversation went something like this.

"Stan, how many work horses have ya got?"

"Four."

"How many saddle horses?"

"Three."

"How many dairy cows'?"

"Thirty head."

"How many beef cattle?"

"Forty head of mama cows and one bull."

"How many hogs?"

"Six sows; one boar."

"Any sheep?"

"Nope."

So it went, through tractors, trucks, trailers, combines, etc. etc.

"Ya got any dogs round here Stan?"

"Nope."

"I thought I saw a dog in the yard a few weeks ago when I drove past."

"Ya might have, but there ain't none around here now."

"Ya got anything else you wanna declare?" Ray was looking at the rifle leaning in the corner of the kitchen!

"Nope."

"Well, I reckon that does it."

With that being said, Raymond packed up and left, after shaking hands, and being given a bag of fresh tomatoes.

Eddie's dad saw the two of us looking at him out of the corner of our eyes. "What's the matter with you two?"

Eddie said, "You told him we didn't own any dogs, and we do!"

"I didn't tell him that"

"I heard you!"

"No, ya didn't. He asked if I had any dogs *"around here?"* and I told him "No" . Go out and look around and tell me if ya find any! Ya won't, because the dog is in town with Jim!"

"Well, he asked you if we had anything else, and you said no! He was looking at the rifle the whole time! He knew you weren't telling the truth!"

"That wasn't what he asked, and I told the truth! He asked if there was anything else that I **wanted** to declare! I said no! Why do ya think he keeps getting re-elected? He knows **how** to ask a question!"

Raymond, the assessor, was actually a nice guy. This was probably why he kept getting re-elected each time he ran for office. Why he wanted the job, I'll never know! It could be a dangerous occupation on occasion! On some occasions, he had been run off by an irate farmer wielding a shotgun! I know this, because I overheard him telling my dad about it. He had some embarrassing moments too. I once overheard him telling Dad about one of them.

The eastern area of the county in which we farmed was slightly rolling with a few hills. However, the western part of the county was nearly flat, with few trees. He told Dad that he had been in that area of the county going his rounds in his car. All of a sudden, he had been gripped with a sudden extreme stomach cramp and a need to go to the toilet. It was so painful, that it required an immediate response. There were no trees or bushes along that section of road. However, the road was deserted, and the nearest farm house was a mile and a half away. Since his need for relief was immediate, he pulled to the side of the gravel road, grabbed some newspaper from his car, and squatted down in the shallow bar-ditch.

He had nearly finished, when he heard the sound of an automobile coming down the road. He could discern that it was occupied by two women. With no cover of any kind, the only thing he could think to do was to throw his shirt tail over his head. His thinking was that with his face covered, they wouldn't know who's rear end was shining in the bar-ditch! The auto honked it's horn and he heard shrill laughter as they passed.

After they had gone, he finished up and returned to his car. To his horror, he saw something he had forgotten about! There, on the side of his car in letters 4 inches high, was the sign that said :

RAYMOND DOZIER
COUNTY ASSESSOR.

Chapter 8

Farm Dogs

Nearly all farmers had a dog or two. Some were just mutts that were kept for their noise making ability when a coyote or other unwelcome visitor came around the chicken pen. Others had a specific purpose. Some, such as coon hounds were kept for the hunting purpose that the name implies. Others were kept to help with herding livestock. My dad always kept border collies. These were intelligent dogs, and through the years we had a number of different ones. Now, a farm was a dangerous place for a dog. Their lives were usually terminated by some accident such as being run over by machinery or other cause. Hence, one dog would replace another. I remember some of them because of certain incidents connected to them. What follows here is an amusing story. Not all of them were!

This incident involved the preacher, or more specifically the preacher's wife. As I have said elsewhere, Sundays were reserved for rest and church. The school house was a white one room structure. On Sundays it also served as the community church. The school desks would be shoved out of the way, and folding chairs would be set up for the congregation. There were about 35 students in the school in all eight grades and about the same number of church people, so space was no problem. In those days, nobody worried much about the separation of church and state! Since the church/school house was about 12 miles from the nearest town, there were no restaurants near by. The preacher lived in a town about 20 miles away. He received no salary. He got enough from the collection plate to pay for his gas, but that was about all.

Since the preacher received no salary, the church deacons (of which my dad was one) decided that various church families should take turns inviting him and his wife to their home for Sunday dinner after church. Thus about once every two months, it was our turn to feed the preacher. These events were always a pain to me, as I was required to be on my best behavior and exhibit my best manners!

On this particular Sunday everything went as usual. It was a warm day and after eating, the preacher and Dad sat on the front porch discussing various topics of the day. I don't really know what they were discussing, as I had taken the first opportunity to make myself absent. The preacher generally spiced his conversation with too many amens and hallelujahs for me.

Later, when I saw that our guests were getting ready to leave, I thought I would put in an appearance. The dog whose name was Pinky, also decided to bid them farewell.

Now, my dad was not prone to using swear words, but he did know some! What happened next proved that even a deacon of the church could be provoked!

As Mom and Dad were shaking hands with preacher and wife, Pinky took a sudden interest in the wife! After some preliminary sniffs around her feet, he suddenly wrapped his front legs around one of her legs and began to hump away like he was on a female dog. She said "ooh, nice doggie, nice doggie, down nice doggie!"

Dad had not been paying any attention to the dog. He now looked down and saw what the dog was doing. He took about three steps and kicked ole Pinky about 10 feet!

"Getouttahere you sonofabitch!" His face turned red! "Oh, sorry preacher!"

Discretion being the better part of valor, I ducked around a corner of the smoke house before laughing. To laugh at that time would not have been a good idea!

Chapter 9
Country Doctors

In the world of the twenty-first century, we have come to accept miracle drugs and a standard of health care that was unheard of during the time frame of this book.

The range of antibiotics that are available to us today, would have truly been considered a miracle in those days. The same is to be said of surgical techniques. This great advance in medical knowledge got it's beginning boost from that unfortunate crime that mankind repeats again and again. This time it was called world war two!

I was born at home in 1938 during the latter part of that period of time known as the "Great Depression". Although there were hospitals in the cities at that time that were considered modern, no one could afford them. The system was quite different from today. As I grew up, I, like most country boys, had my share of broken bones, cuts, and other miscellaneous calamities, that today would require at least a trip to an emergency room! I never saw either a hospital or an emergency room until I was more than 22 years old!

In those days our health care was provided by the "family doctor". They were all men. Some were elderly. Some were middle aged. None were young! The young doctors were all in the military from 1942 until 1946! These "general practitioners" handled everything from ingrown toenails to childbirth and everything in between.

There were several of these men in the town located about twelve miles from our farm. They all had private rented offices. Most of these were located on the upper floors of the two bank buildings in town. They all "made rounds" twice a day in the two local hospitals, where surgical and other patients needing full time nursing care were occupying beds. After they had made these "morning rounds", they would receive patients at their office until "evening rounds", unless a phone call requested their immediate services elsewhere. After these evening rounds, they drove into the countryside to visit their rural patients. When people went to the doctor's office, it was for something that wasn't urgent! Most of these were such things as "female complaints" or a boil on the backside, etc. etc. Urgent problems resulted in a call from the patients home! There were no prior appointments. Sometimes, if you went to the office, you were told by his nurse, that, "doctor is attending a sick patient!" This meant that he was at someone's home, or at the hospital. No one knew when he would be back!

In looking back, I can't understand how they were able to withstand the time demands that their chosen profession made upon them! When called, they came! Whether it was two o'clock in the afternoon or two hours after midnight, they always came to the frantic call from a mother who said, "my child is running a high fever, and I don't know what else to do!" They came in all weather! In blinding rain and lightning and in driving snow, with the thermometer at ten below zero! I can remember the relief in my mom's voice, "Thank God", when in the dark of night, my dad would say "the Doc's here!"

These superb, totally dedicated men were the last of the "Horse and Buggy" doctors, except that they traveled by automobile! During the war, they did not have ration cards for gas, as nearly everyone else did! They had a special card that exempted them from the ration. They didn't receive a lot of pay during the depression years! The price for my birth was $5.00 plus 6 chickens! It took 3 months for my dad to pay the total amount of the cash!

Warren Galloway was our family doctor. He delivered me at birth. He was my doctor until I moved out of the state twenty six years later. Although he was only five or six years older than my dad, I always thought of him as old Doc Galloway.

Doc Galloway was the epitome of the country doctor! He could be brusque; telling a teenage boy that he thought was malingering in order to get out of work, "Get out of bed. What you need is exercise!" He could be gentle when the occasion required. He was a superb surgeon who had studied four years in Germany. At the time, German surgeons were considered the best in the world! He, at one time, served on the examining board of the Kansas Medical Society.

Sometime after I was born, Doc Galloway purchased some farm land near us. He asked Dad if he would farm it on shares. My dad agreed, and farmed the place for the next several years. During this time, Doc and my dad became good friends, and remained so after Dad no longer farmed Doc's property.

Doc was always in a hurry! The demands on his time were severe, causing him to move at a rapid pace. This was especially so when he was in his automobile, roaring from one house call to the next. In those days, in Kansas there were no speed limits outside the towns. This suited Doc just fine, because he always drove at one speed. Full throttle! Therein lies a story, I once heard a local lawman tell my dad.

Doc always drove a big Packard automobile. The Packard was a car noted for its power and speed. It was very heavy. The car weighed over 4,000 pounds and would run in excess of 90 miles per hour.

There was a small burg about eight miles outside the town where Doc had his office. The paved highway ran straight through the town. The little town was no more than a half mile from city limit to city limit.

The business section consisted of a gas station, a café and a grain elevator. It was policed by a city Marshall. There was a speed limit of thirty miles per hour through the town.

On the day of this story, the Marshall had been parked in the gas station, when a big Packard came past, as the Marshall said, "flying low". He immediately gave chase. When the driver of the Packard saw the red light behind him, he pulled to the side of the road and stopped. When the Marshall approached the car, he discovered the driver was Doc Galloway! The Marshall told my dad the conversation went as follows.

"Doc, you were goin' a little fast weren't ya?"

"How fast was I going?"

"About seventy five!"

"I guess I need to get this thing tuned up. It oughta do better than that!"

"Doc, I'm goin' to have to give ya a ticket."

"How much is it gonna cost me?"

"About ten bucks!"

Doc pulled a twenty dollar bill from his wallet.

"Here Marshall. Keep it all!"

"Why should I do that?"

"Because when I come back thru here, I'm gonna be going the same damned way! And I don't have time to stop again!"

Chapter 10
A Dollars Worth

It is necessary, to make some comments about the value of money in the time span that this book covers.

The consumer of today, when the (so-called) median income is $30,000.00, will not believe a time that a dollar had the purchasing power that I am listing below! These are not depression prices, but in 1950-1952 in a robust economy! Here are some examples of average prices in Kansas at that time!

New 3 bedroom, 1 ½ bath home $8,000 to $12,000
New Chevrolet Auto $1,400 to $2, 000
Regular Gasoline   14.9 cents per Gal.
Hamburger (we didn't buy it)   33.3 cents per Lb.
Bread (we didn't buy it)   15 to 20 C. per loaf
Cigarettes $1.10 per carton
Federal minimum wage $0.75 per hour
Men's hair cuts   50 cents to $1.00

Hired farm labor was even lower priced than the federal minimum wage. A married hired farm hand, who had what was considered a good job, was paid about $100.00 per month. However, he was furnished a house rent free, a garden spot for his wife, and allowed to raise a hundred chickens, using the farmers grain to feed them. He was allowed to have a milk cow of his own. He was also usually given a hog to butcher each year. There were no taxes withheld from his wages! At this time, farm labor was exempt from withholding and social security taxes! My folks always treated our hired hand and his family as if they were a part of our family. Unmarried farm hands were not desirable, as they were usually transients, who would quit when the work got hard!

My dad didn't pay for everything with coin of the realm! During the war years, when nearly everything, including flour, and coal, was rationed, a barter system sprang up and continued on after the war was over! It worked like this.

Every year at wheat harvest, Dad would haul a pickup load of wheat to a small local mill about 15 miles away. It was an old fashioned mill, that was operated by water power. (It is still there, although, it is now a tourist attraction.) The mill was operated by an elderly gentleman who was a first generation Scot, unlike my father, who was third generation! I was present once and I think they both enjoyed the encounter! The conversation between them went something like this.

"Aye, William Ross, I see that ye've brought me some more second class wheat, ye wish ta trade for my good flour!"

"Well, Mac, I ain't sure I do!"

"Whyn't ?"

"Depends on the bargain!"

"Well, laddie, lemme take a better look at yer grain"

"Help yerself."

MacDonald would then make a show of inspecting the grain. Running it through his fingers and peering at the grain in his hand, he would say: "It's somat bleached, un there's quite a lot shriveled! T'wont weigh more than 55"

"It weighs 60 pounds! I had it checked and cleaned at the elevator before I brought it over!"

"Did ye now? Well , yere a good boy ! Yere daddy wast a good friend o'me when I got here!" (to the USA) He then dropped the Scottish brogue because his normal speech sounded just like ours! "I'll let ya have 22."

"40"

"25"

"35"

"27, and it's me last offer!"

"30, or I'm leavin"

"Done and done. Put er on the scales!"

"Bill, pull on the scales."

I followed Dad's instruction and weighed and dumped the wheat. We had hauled in 50 bushels of 60 pound wheat. The total amount was just over 3,000 pounds. What this meant, was that my dad had a credit at the mill for 1500 pounds of the mill's products.

The negotiation had been settled that we would receive 30 pounds of flour, corn meal, rolled oats, or other products for each 60 pounds of wheat we had delivered. Both men knew where this would end up, but neither could forsake his Scottish ancestry!

During the months until next wheat harvest, when Mom's supplies ran low, Dad would go to the mill and pick up the necessary items! The mill kept track of how much was in his account, and how much he had used.

Another item that my dad bartered for was coal. We always cut wood in the fall months! The wood we cut was placed in a large pile behind the house. Since the wood was generally green when it was cut, it was allowed to cure and dry for a year while we used last year's cutting.

Kansas winters are unpredictable. They can be mild or brutal! Dad always backed up our wood supply with coal! Each summer, in August, he went to town to buy the winters supply. Depending on the price of coal and the market price of animals and the amount of coal he wanted, he would trade butchered meat for the coal. This could range from half a hog, to a full hog, or a half a beef!

This system worked well! The coal dealer purchased his meat at a lesser price than retail, and Dad got his coal at a lower cost! There were no middle men's profits involved!

In that bygone era gasoline was purchased at "service" stations. Gas was not sold by indifferent clerks in a "quick trip" grocery! When a potential customer drove up beside the gas pumps, one and sometimes two attendants immediately came out to the vehicle. While the customer sat in comfort inside the vehicle, they would check the air in the tires, check the oil level in the engine and wash the windshield! Then the driver would be politely asked what else he or she needed. The customer would reply in a firm manner! "Gimme a dollars worth!"

Chapter 11

Guests

One Monday morning at breakfast, Dad looked across the table at me. "Son, after breakfast, I would like you to fuel up the Case and the Ford tractor and grease the mowing machines. Herbert, do you have anything urgent to do today?"

"Not that I know of"

"Good! I want you to help Bill fuel the tractors, and hook up the mowing machines. The weather is good, and with an early start, the alfalfa field can be mowed today. You and Bill can get it done if you use both mowers."

"I don't know how to mow hay."

"Bill will show you how."

With that said, Dad arose from the table, put on his cap, and leaving the house, got in the pick-up truck and drove off. Herbert sat at the table with a nonplused look on his face.

I said, "Well Herbert, we better get to it" I understood that "I would like" was a direct order!

Herbert asked; "What should I wear?"

"What ever you want, It's going to be pretty hot in that hay field." With this, I stood up, put on my cap and went outside to begin carrying out Dad's instructions.

I was about half finished fueling the second tractor, when Herbert made his appearance. He was dressed much as I had been; in a tee shirt and denim jeans. Dad required that everyone wear a shirt while in the house. Also, your hair must be combed, and no caps were allowed! Immediately after leaving the house however, I had removed my tee shirt. This far into the summer, my upper body was tanned the color of leather due to sun exposure. Herbert, seeing that I had removed my shirt, elected to do the same.

Some explanation is due the reader.

My mom was the youngest of twelve siblings. She had one sister that had survived childhood. The rest were brothers. Thus, I had a large herd of cousins on that side of the family. Herbert was a member of that herd. Mom's brothers were a mixed bag! Some were upright citizens of their communities, and some (to quote my dad) "weren't worth the powder and lead it would take to blow them to hell." Herbert was the twenty five year old son of one of the latter, and a chip off the old block!

Herbert and his wife had arrived unannounced (on vacation they said) three weeks prior to the aforesaid Monday morning. As family of course, they were invited to stay and partake of our humble fare. This they did with gusto! Now, my mother was one of those women who made sure that no one ever left her table hungry! I have wondered about Herbert and wife, however, because they ate every doggone morsel in sight! I believe they enjoyed their extended "vacation" because they never left the place!

Herbert spent his days in the hammock in the front yard; leaving it only to answer the call of nature, or to inquire when supper was going to be ready! As it turned out, he was "between jobs, and spending time considering his next career move." This, according to his wife.

Back to Monday!

About nine o'clock, we got to the hay field after I showed Herbert how to drive the small tractor. Or rather, after placing it in the gear suitable for mowing, and showing him the clutch, throttle and pto shift lever. At this age, (14) I took the large tractor. After about an hour of hit and miss, Herbert got straightened out and did a fairly good job of steering the tractor. This was all that was really required in the flat, square, thirty acre field, once the speed of the machine was set.

When we went to the house at noon, Dad had returned. I retrieved my shirt, washed my face and hands on the back porch, removed my cap, combed my hair, donned my shirt, and went into the house. Herbert followed suit, except, he didn't put his shirt on. In only three hours exposure to the Kansas sun, he looked like a boiled lobster!

Dad was at the table when we came into the house. To Herbert; "Where's your shirt?"

"My back is kinda' sore."

"Well, it should be. You can't go that long in the sun without a shirt."

"Bill did."

"He's used to it. Get a shirt on. No one is allowed at the table without a shirt. Then, sit down, so we can say Grace. The foods getting cold."

It was punishment of course! Dad had become irritated with Herbert's lackadaisical, freeloading attitude. Herbert had not once asked if he could help us with field work that was going on the entire time he had been there! Dad had decided that a lesson about hard work was in order!

We finished mowing that afternoon, and Herbert went to the pond with Dad and I to bathe. Afterward, when we had eaten, and Mom had rubbed his sunburned skin with juice from her medicine plant (aloe), he went directly to bed.

The next morning, the medicine plant had done it's work, and Herbert was feeling pretty chipper until Dad ruined his breakfast!

"Son, we didn't pick up any moisture last night. So we can rake and bale fairly early today."

I now found out where Dad had gone the morning before. "I talked to Elton yesterday. He and the two boys are bringing a rake and two bale trailers over this morning. Howard Russell and his boy are bringing one bale trailer. Stan Outerbine can't come, but he is sending a bale trailer over with Jim and Eddy. This, with Herbert will give us ten men." (In those days a teenage boy over twelve was equated as a man) "I'm going to put Herbert on the bale trailer with you, behind the baler. Eddie Outerbine can haul the trailers to the barn, since he's the smallest one. Herbert, you can hang around up here until we start baling."

Herbert looked downcast. I was elated !

It is necessary for me to explain why I was elated.

At this time, we had a new self tying hay baler. This was a machine at the forefront of the new age in farm machinery. This machine used twine, not wire. After the hay had been rolled into "windrows" by "side delivery" hay rakes, the baler was pulled down each windrow by a tractor, feeding the hay into the baling mechanism. Behind the baler was towed a bale trailer. This was a four wheeled wagon on rubber tires, that had a short "tongue". The baler had an inclined chute, that delivered the baled hay to the front of the bale trailer. Each bale weighed about 70 pounds. The hay handler on the bale trailer had a job that provided no rest, as long as the baler was operating. In good hay, the bales came out of the chute at a rate of three per minute! The trailer man had enough time to grab the new bale with his hay hook, drag it back and stack it up to three tiers high on the trailer. When he returned, there was another bale waiting! The only rest for the trailer man came while the trailers were being changed.

Since it was our baler, my dad always operated the baler. From the age of fourteen on, I was always the "man" on the bale trailer. The reader can understand why I was elated that there were going to be two people on the bale trailer, instead of only me!

Well, we started baling about one o'clock that afternoon. I, of course, was bucking hay on the bale trailer, behind the baler. Right along beside me was ole Herbert! He didn't do all that bad! His numbers were about three to my five. When the hay started to get tough, we quit at about 7.00 p.m. We had baled close to a thousand bales in that six hours.

Dad said "Well, we can finish it tomorrow if it doesn't rain." We all went to the pond, bathed, returned, ate, and were in bed by nine o'clock. My mom and sister had done the chores.

The next morning at breakfast, Herbert and his wife were absent. Dad said to Mom. "Where's Herbert and Angie?" Mom replied; "Well, they left around ten o'clock, after you had gone to bed."

"Why did they leave at that time of night?"

"As Angie explained it to me , Herbert had a career offer in Tulsa Oklahoma, that required him to be there today!"

"What kind of a career?"

"I don't know. I think it was partly caused by a conversation that I had with her yesterday."

"What did you say?"

"Well, she asked me what you were paying Herbert for his hard work. I told her that you considered anyone to be guests up to two weeks. After that, you considered them boarders, who had to work for their room and board!"

I kinda missed ole Herbert that day! We baled the remaining 800 bales in the field. I stacked every danged one of them on the trailers! If Herbert had of been there, he would've handled at least 200!

Chapter 12
Hunting Elusive Snipe

It was a lazy Sunday afternoon later in the same summer that Crawdad Russell had earned his nickname. Five of us were sitting on our front porch trying to think of something to do to occupy the time before evening chore time. The group consisted of myself, Jim Outerbine, Denny Miller, Elmo Russell, (who by now everyone called Crawdad), and my cousin, Kenny. We were all about the same age, with me being 2 weeks older than Jim, who was a month older than Denny, who was 2 months older than Crawdad. The exception was Kenny, who was a year older than me. We used our slight age difference to boss Crawdad, whose dad had taught to "respect your elders." Crawdad was big enough to break any of us in two pieces, but he was a gentle giant, whose good nature we constantly took advantage of.

Little did we know at this time, that in less than 5 years two of the four would be dead. One to be killed in a car accident and the other to be killed in a hunting accident!

But, on this Sunday afternoon we were just four good ole boys plus one city boy with nothing to do. For about 4 summers Kenny had come from Kansas City, where he lived, to spend four to six weeks on the farm. This was my uncle Archie's idea. Uncle Archie was a Presbyterian minister. Kenny proved the old adage about preacher's sons. He wasn't mean. He was good natured! He was always respectful of my parents and other older people. But he was ready to try anything, which made him a perfect victim for a bunch of "good ole boys."

Jim winked at me. "Hey, lets have a snipe hunt"

Crawdad grinned. "Hooboy !"

"Pipe down Crawdad! Have ya ever hunted snipe, Kenny?"

"No I ain't, but I'd like to try it."

Crawdad, "Hooboy !"

"Well, yer in luck. Snipe season opened last week, and they ain't been hunted yet."

He looked at the rest of us for confirmation. We all nodded our heads to solemnly confirm that this was true!

"I ain't gotta a gun!"

"Ya don't need one! The only things ya need are a burlap sack and a stick. Down in the pasture there's a ditch, the snipe use for a runway."

"Yeah, I know the ditch yer talkin about. It is about four feet wide and a couple of feet deep. Sometimes it's got water in it."

"Ya ain't gonna have to worry about that now. We ain't had a rain in a couple a weeks."

Kenny was then given the complete plan. It went as follows. Since the snipe lived in the pasture, but used the ditch as a pathway to their nests, Kenny would take the sack and the stick and hide in the ditch. The ditch was about a quarter mile long. The rest of us would go to the other end of the ditch and make a lot of noise. That would rattle the birds so much that they would run down the ditch. As they fled in blind panic from the noise, they would pass by where Kenny was hidden. He was to whack them in the head with the stick, and drop them in the bag!

"Won't they fly when they see me and the bag?"

"No, they're like an ostrich, 'cept not as big. They can't fly. If ya sit perfectly still, they won't notice ya until they're within th' reach of th' stick!"

So it went! We left Kenny in the ditch at one side of the pasture while we drove around to the other side. We immediately set up such a racket, that my dad heard it from the house, which was only about 200 yards from where we were. Our noise immediately spooked some of the cattle, and caused Dad to walk out to see what we were doing. When he asked "What are you ornery boys up to?" We told him that we were on a snipe hunt. He looked at us and asked, "Who's holdin' the bag"?

I said "Kenny is".

He shook his head, said "lower the noise, you're scarin' the cattle," and went back to the house. Now, the pasture wasn't perfectly level. It had some small rises, and dips in it. After about an hour, Kenny appeared, walking in the ditch which meandered back and forth. He found the four of us lying on the grass taking a nap!

Denny said "Where's th' birds? Yer sack looks empty!"

"None came past!"

"You're kiddin' , we made enough noise to wake th' dead!"

Crawdad said "Hooboy!"

"Well," I said "it's almost time to do chores. Those cattle runnin' around must have scared them out into the grass. Lets come back at dark, when the cows will be penned in the barn lot." Everyone agreed that this was a good idea!

That night was a repeat of the daytime hunt, except that this time when Kenny returned, he found us in the machine shop, throwing darts at a dart board!

The story should end there. But it doesn't!! The next Sunday, on the front porch, someone again suggested we go snipe hunting. The person making the suggestion was Kenny!

I wonder if later in life, anyone ever told Kenny where the phrase "left holding the bag" came from! None of us ever did!

Chapter 13
Outhouses

It was Halloween night after my sixteenth birthday. The four good ole boys; me, Jim, Denny, and Crawdad, were sitting on our horses about a half mile outside of the little town considering our plans for the night. The town was located about eight miles from where we lived. However, Jim's dad had a half section of rented pasture about two miles down the road. That afternoon we had loaded our four saddle horses into two horse trailers and hauled them to the barn located on the pasture. After dark we had returned, saddled the horses, and were now ready for the fun to begin!

Let me assure the readers! We were not mean boys! We didn't destroy property! We didn't scare people, (well, leastwise, not elderly people and little kids)! Like many of our escapades, this foray could be blamed indirectly on our dads. This was because we got a lot of our ideas by listening to them reminisce about pranks they had pulled when they were boys!

The outdoor toilet has several names. It is called the "privy", "outhouse", "two holer", and other, less polite names. The school house toilets were about six feet square. Most private ones were about four feet square. They were of two basic types.

The first type was called a "Roosevelt". It was so named, because, during the Roosevelt administration the government had created a public works program. It's purpose was to create jobs for the unemployed. Someone administering the program got the idea of constructing outdoor toilets on farms that were more sanitary than the existing ones. This "killed two birds with one stone" so to speak. It created work for men and improved the farm family's health at government expense. These little structures had a pre-cast concrete stool and floor. The stool (or commode if you prefer) had a wood seat with a lid. It also had a wood vent duct that ran from the stool up through the roof. The little building sat over a concrete lined pit.

The second type was the original "privy". It had a wood floor and a wood bench seat. This seat usually had two holes; a small one for children and a larger one for adults! These sat over an earthen pit that was about four to six feet deep. They didn't have a vent pipe through the roof. The vent pipe, or lack of one , told you which type it was.

The "Roosevelt" type were bolted to the their concrete floor. The others merely sat over their pit. Two men could easily push over, one of these latter types. This did not tear them up. They could be stood upright with very little trouble!

Quite a bit of planning had gone into this foray! We were all dressed in dark colored clothes. We had come equipped for the night. Each boy had a lariat, a slingshot, and a sack full of torpedoes. These torpedoes had the same loud boom that 2 inch firecrackers had. They didn't have a fuse. They exploded on impact!

The little town of around 400 people was laid out in square city blocks about 300 by 300 feet. Each block had an alley running through the middle. The business section faced the main street for a length of about 2 blocks with various business enterprises on each side. There was a grain elevator at one end and a lumber yard at the other. It was a mostly modern little town.

Some years before, the city council had held a referendum vote by the citizens of the town. The overwhelming vote, was to have a city water and sewer system. There was a minority that voted against it because it was funded by monthly fees for water and sewer charged by the city. The measure was adopted. However, it had a flaw. It allowed property owners to opt out of the system. Property owners could continue using outdoor toilets, and could use water from private wells if they chose to do so. There were a few hardheads who thought it was "damned foolish" to pay the town for water, when they could pump it from their private well for free and use their own outhouse for free All of the business buildings had modern facilities, except one! Of course, the hardheads also had privies on the alley behind their house.

The local law consisted of a town Marshall, who had vowed publicly that he was "going to collar any danged kids that caused any mischief on Halloween night!" He hadn't thought about saddle horses!

The plan was this! About eleven o'clock when most of the town had gone to sleep, we would ride quietly up and down the alleys, and tip over any "two-holers" we found. Only three were owned by elderly people. Between the four of us, we knew everyone in town, so we knew which ones these were. These, we wouldn't bother. The tip over was accomplished by a very simple method! We merely fastened each end of a lariat to the saddle horns of two horses. We then rode a horse past each side of the privy with the rope hanging between them. The rope would come tight against one side of the little building. When it did so, a slight nudge of the heels, and the building would topple.

The plan worked perfectly! The occasional barking of the few dogs in town, aroused no one! The toppling of the little buildings created little noise. It was just a "thud" that awoke no one to see what was going on. The Marshall drove up and down the streets in his Studebaker car, but we easily evaded him as the town only had four street lights. These were located on main street.

It was close to one o'clock when we rode into the alley behind the business buildings on main street. We saw the Marshall's car sitting in the lumberyard parking lot at the other end of the block. The parking lot was lighted. The Marshall could be clearly seen sitting in the car. We were in the dark alley! It was impossible for him to see us in return! After watching him for some time, Jim said "I think he's asleep!" Handing me the reins to his horse, "I'm goin' to check it out!"

We watched as Jim crept down the alley, and crawled up behind the car! "He's gonna get caught!"

"Crawdad, be quiet!" in a whisper.

As we watched, Jim peeked in the rear window of the car. We saw him squat down by the right rear tire. After a minute or so, he crawled away from the car, into the shadows, and sneaked back up the alley to where we were standing. "I was right. He's asleep!" As he said this, he opened his hand. Laying in his palm, shiny and bright, was the valve stem core from the rear tire! Our plan had been to shoot the torpedoes into the main street with the sling shots, to keep the Marshall's attention. Now there would be no need! As it turned out, Jim's daring paid off; for we were about to have a disaster!

The building behind which we were hiding was the general store. It was a holdover from much earlier days! The owner, whose name was Burch, was also a holdover. He sold everything from dynamite to saddles to thread and needles.

He was a hardheaded, but well liked, old gentlemen. He also had the only privy behind a business building! He had said "This year, no darned kids are goin' to push over my outhouse!" We soon discovered why he had said this.

His privy sat about three feet from the main building. Across this space, about six feet above the ground, he had fastened two 2x4 boards. These were in turn, fastened to the main building. A horse couldn't go under these boards. To us, however, it was a challenge!

I handed my reins to Denny. "Hold my horse Denny. Crawdad, get off your horse and give the reins to Jim."

"What're we goin' to do?"

"You'll see." as I shinnied myself up between the two buildings.

"Get up here beside me." Crawdad did as he was told (always). We were now above the 2X4 boards, with our backs against the large building, and our feet against the wall of the privy. "Crawdad, do exactly what I tell you, when I tell you!"

"Okay."

"Push!" The little building began to move and the boards tore loose with a crash! The privy toppled! "Jump!" When I yelled this, I jumped to one side! Crawdad jumped straight ahead! (and down!)

He lucked out! The pit under the privy had been there for so long, that all but the top eighteen inches, or so had turned to compost. He did manage to sink in to his knees!

Several things now happened simultaneously!

#1 Elmo yelled at the top of his voice. "gimmeouttahere!"

#2 The town Marshall woke up!

#3 Elmo's racket spooked the horses! They began to rear up!

While Jim and Denny tried to handle the horses, I grabbed Crawdad's hand and yanked him out of the pit! We heard the Marshall start his car! Then, rummmm, rummmm from his engine! Then, thump, thump, thump, as he started to move. He stopped, got out of his car; and upon seeing his flat tire, let out a string of cuss words, that would have made a sailor blush!

By this time everyone except Elmo, was mounted. His horse didn't like his odor one bit! However, he finally got the horse to see things his way, and we headed out of town at a dead run!

We got to the barn and put the horses up. Calling it a successful night, we headed home. Crawdad had ridden over to the barn with me. I made him ride home in the back of the pickup!

Chapter 14

Farm Women

Today, farm women are able to have the same conveniences as the women living in the city. It was not always so!

Just as the farmer's life was changed by the introduction of electricity to rural America, his wife's was also! After electricity was available, my mom's life changed to a large degree. Even, after this, her daily work routine would appall most of the women of today.

When I think of the life my mother led in those days, I am reminded of an old adage, that went like this.

A farmers work is from sun to sun.

His wife's work is never done!

Some of this was caused by my parent's attitude about spending money. Dad was of pure Scottish descent, and my mom was Scots/German. They were not miserly. They were very thrifty!

Mom's day began at five o'clock in the morning. This was every day, with no exceptions! On a farm, the daily chores went on every day of the week, no matter what else was happening! Dad would arise at four o'clock, and in the winter, build up the fire, in the wood heating stove. Mom would get up an hour later. From the age of 13 on, I got up at the same time. I dressed, and followed Dad to the milk barn to help with the chores.

While I was doing this, Mom began preparations for breakfast. This was no simple chore! Although, I have no memory of it, during the depression years Mom cooked on a wood stove. Kerosene cook stoves were available, but no one could afford the kerosene fuel. Kerosene was reserved for the lamps! Even in later years, Mom had the same attitude toward cooking! Everything was made from "scratch"!

Mom baked fresh biscuits every morning! Along with these, she prepared ham, bacon or sausage with eggs and fried potatoes. Once in a great while, she would fix fried mush, which Dad loved and I hated! We topped the biscuits with gravy or homemade jam or honey and butter. Everything she used, except the salt and baking soda, came from the farm. While we were eating, water would be heating in the teakettle. As soon as breakfast was over, she and my sister, Sue would wash the dishes . During the school year I would change my clothes and Sue and I left for school.

If it was a Monday, Mom would then haul any soiled clothes and linens out to the wash house. This was a little building about 12 feet wide, and 20 feet long. It stood about 30 feet from the rear porch. Inside, was a wood cook stove, the washing machine, and three round steel tubs. One tub sat on the stove, and two on wooden stands. Mom used the wood stove to heat wash water, which she dipped from the tub on the stove into the washing machine and the other two "rinse" tubs'. First Dad, and then later I carried cold water into the wash house from the well, if we were not out in the field.

When Mom had a sufficient supply of hot water, she would start the washing machine. She was very proud of this machine! It was a Maytag brand with a square tub. At the rear, two "wringers" were located. It had a little, one cylinder gasoline engine, that was started by a kick pedal. Mom would add soap in the washer and dump in the clothes, after sorting them according to color. White clothes and sheets were washed separately from colored items.

After she deemed that everything had washed sufficiently, she would shift the machine "agitator" out of gear and engage the wringers. These wringers were power driven rubber rollers that would squeeze the water out, when the clothes were fed between them. The first pass through into the first rinse tub, squeezed the soapy wash water out. She then stirred the items around in the first tub to rinse them. Then, everything was run through the wringers into the second tub and rinsed again. Finally, the clothes were run through them a third time and placed in a basket, to be carried outside to the clothes line for drying. Mom washed in this manner long after we had electricity!

Wash day was always on Monday except when it was storming outside. Freezing weather was not considered a deterrent! I have seen Mom, wearing a heavy coat, and hanging clothes on the clothes line when they were freezing dry in less than an hour! If there was a storm, wash day would be exchanged with baking day! Ironing day was always the day after wash day.

My parents didn't buy bread at the grocery store or bakery! Mom baked bread every week. Usually on Wednesday.

Bread baking day was my favorite day of the week! The aroma that greeted my nose when I came home from school, or in from the field always made my mouth water! Mom not only baked bread, she baked cinnamon rolls and made doughnuts! I have never in my adult life tasted any bakery goods that had the delicious flavor of my mom's baking! She knew this. In later years, after my dad had died, she would bake bread and make doughnuts when she knew I was coming home for a visit!   In addition to the baking, ironing, washing, mending, and cooking, Mom kept a large garden. From her garden came all the vegetables we ate. In summer these would be fresh. In the winter they would be canned. We had a root cellar in which we stored the things that Mom had preserved during the summer. In the root cellar there were such things as tomatoes, carrots, peas, green beans, hominy, corn, peaches, pears, pickles and all manner of things packed in glass jars, as well as kraut in stone jars, potatoes on racks, and any other food item that needed to be protected from both heat, and cold.

Mom took care of the chickens, and the garden (with some help from Sue and myself). She did the chores when all the men were in the field late! When all of the summer tasks were done, and winter cold had set in, she used the time to sew shirts for Dad and I, dresses for herself and my sister, knit sweaters for us, and crochet table scarves and doilies.

In addition to all the work that she did, Mom also found time to care for the health of her family. Most of her home remedies had one of three things in common. They tasted awful, felt awful, or smelled bad! When I caught a cold, her favorite remedy was one I hated most! It was called an onion poultice. It was made by frying two or three chopped up onions, which were then sewn inside a flat muslin sack. The whole thing was then strapped to my chest, overnight. It worked! I don't know why. Maybe it was the fumes, from the onions in my lungs. Maybe germs couldn't stand the smell any more than I could! Mom not only cured us, she comforted us when we were unhappy.

In our school, most of the students were country kids, who lived in the same manner that we did. When I was in the first grade, a family from the city moved into a rental house in our district. They said they wanted their children to have "the country experience!" They were not wealthy. The husband worked on the railroad.

Their kids, however, were less than thrilled with "the country experience." There was a boy in the fourth grade, a third grade girl, and a pair of twin girls in the second grade. They referred to the rest of us as "hicks". They were always dressed in store bought clothes.

Most of my shirts had been sewn by my mother from 100 lb. flour sacks. The flour mill where my dad traded, sacked their flour in light cotton sacks, with a colorful checkered pattern on them. My mother, being a thrifty person, as well as an excellent seamstress, made them into shirts! When I wore holes in the knees of my pants, she patched them with material from trousers that I had outgrown. This practice led to the following little story and some advice from my mother, that I have remembered all my life!

One day, when I came home from school, Mom was at the sink. She could see that something was bothering me. She asked, "What's wrong Billy?"

"Nuthin"

"I know there is. What is it?"

"Th' Harlan twins were makin' fun of me!" as I broke into tears.

"Cmere and tell me about it," as she dried her hands, and sat down on a kitchen chair. In the first grade, I was small for my age, and could easily climb on to my mom's lap.

"Well, its my clothes!" as I climbed up to be comforted.

"What's wrong with your clothes?"

"My shirts are homemade!"

"Don't you like your shirts,?"

"Yeah, but---!"

"But what?"

"They said you were too poor, or stingy to buy my shirts!"

Mom sat for a moment with a thoughtful look on her face.

"Sonny, we're not poor!" (Indeed, we were not. My parents had prospered after the depression. Our farm had grown from 160 acres to 480.) "We are not stingy either! I make your shirts because I love you, and It makes me feel good to make things for you and your father! Don't you want me to have this pleasure? If you like your shirts, that is all that matters! Don't worry about those dumb kids! Did they say anything else?"

"Yeah, they did!"

"What about?"

"They said I had patches on my knees, and I do!"

After another moment of thought, she said, *"Billy, always remember this! There is no shame in patches, as long as they're* **clean** *patches!"*

Chapter 15
Home Brew

Pow! The sound was muffled. We were sitting at the big table in the kitchen, to eat supper. Dad had just finished saying Grace. Dad looked at Mom. "I think you've capped your root beer too soon. That came from the root cellar!"

"I haven't made any root beer lately."

"Well, that sounded like something blowing up in the root cellar! After supper we'll have a look."

My brother, Merle looked across the table at me. I looked down at my plate! We both knew what it was!

Merle was seventeen at the time. I was seven. I admired him, as most little brother's do. I generally knew about his antics and wouldn't tattle on him under any circumstance!

Merle had been over at uncle Harley's house, a few days before. This was what had led to the present situation in the root cellar!

Uncle Harley lived in an extra house my dad had acquired when he purchased a small adjoining farm. In lieu of rent, he worked part time as a hired hand. While Dad was a thrifty Scot, his brother-in-law was a congenial, free spending man of the world! Merle and I liked to visit his house because he could tell amazing stories! Also, because aunt Delphi made great lemon pies! On the last visit, Merle had mentioned that he liked Mom's root beer.

Uncle Harley had said, "I make my drink like that, but it tastes better than root beer!"

"What's it taste like?"

"I've got some in the cellar. Would ya like to taste it?"

"You bet!"

Uncle Harley went down into his root cellar, and returned with two soda pop bottles that had been sealed with corks. He pulled the cork out of each one, and offered one bottle to Merle. After drinking some of his bottle, Merle agreed that he liked it better than root beer!

"How do ya make it?"

"Same way yer mom makes root beer, only with different stuff!" He then proceeded to give Merle the recipe. "Be sure to store it in a cool place!"

"I ain't got any corks."

"Ya don't need em. Yer mom use's a metal bottle capper. Ya can use that!"

"What's this stuff called?"

"Home brew, but I wouldn't tell yer dad about it!"

"Why?"

"He don't like the flavor. He's kinda funny that way!"

A few days later, Merle decided to try out uncle Harley's recipe. He remembered what uncle Harley had said about Dad, and decided he would make the brew in the milk barn, and store it under the potato bin, in the root cellar. Every thing went as planned, and he stored twenty bottles of the mixture in the root cellar. This had been three or four days before the explosion gave his plan away!

After supper, we all went out to the root cellar that was located only a short distance from the house. The cellar had two doors. The first was just above ground level, and set at a slope. It hinged upward to reveal a stairway leading downward to the second door. This door hinged inward, and led to three more steps leading down to the floor of the cellar. At the rear of the cellar, was the potato bin. This was a wooden shelf about thirty inches above the floor. The bottom of the bin was constructed of wooden slats, with about ½ inch gap between them. This allowed air to circulate around the potatoes. Under this bin was where Merle had stashed his bottles of home brew.

When Dad opened the first door, a sour yeast smell greeted our noses. Going down the stairway, Dad started to open the second door. Just as the door was open about six inches, POW, another explosion went off! This one wasn't muffled!

Dad jerked the door closed. He turned and frowned at Merle! A thing that always amazed me about Dad, was that he was so wise!

"How many of those did ya put in there?"

"Who, me?"

"Don't be cute! How many?"

"Twenty." (hanging his head)

"When did ya put em there?"

"Three or four days ago."

"So there's about a dozen and a half left. Is that right?"

"Yeah."

"I should send ya down there now, but I won't, because its too dangerous! Ya might get hit with flying glass!"

"Okay." (with relief)

"Where did ya get the idea of making that stuff?"

"Uncle Harley gave me the recipe. He said you didn't like the taste of it, so I didn't tell you! It's called----"

Dad; (cutting him off.) "I know what it's called, and I better not catch ya making any more of it! You're gonna get to clean the mess up, when it quits exploding! Meanwhile, don't anyone go in there until I say it's okay! Merle, ya can forget goin' to town for the next couple of Saturday nights! "Leatha, I'm goin' to have a little talk with that brother of your's!"

About ten days later, after the explosions had ceased, ole Merle spent an entire day cleaning up the root cellar! He never did like home brew after that!

Chapter 16
Rustlers!

They say that all families have at least one black sheep. This is not to say that mine had only one. Due to the large herd of cousins that I had, my mom's family had more than it's share!

I was only 5 years old at the time, and only have hazy memories of the following story. However, my dad related it to me many times.

One morning in 1943, when Dad went to the milking barn to begin milking, he noticed that the door to the horse barn was open. This didn't really disturb him, because all the horses were locked in individual box stalls inside the barn. When my brother, Merle arrived a short time later, Dad told him to go shut the door. Merle came running back to the milking barn a few minutes later. "Dad, one of the saddle horses is gone!"

"He probably just got out of his stall and nudged the barn door open."

"His saddle and bridle are missing too!"

"Finish up the milking, I'm going to the horse barn!"

By this time, there was enough daylight to see into the cattle holding pen beyond the barn. Dad saw that the gate leading to the county road from the holding pen was open! There had been three cows in the holding pen the previous evening. Now, there wasn't a cow in sight! Dad took off at a fast walk to the house.

He entered the kitchen and immediately went to the phone. Mom heard him ring the operator and ask for the Sheriff's office. While waiting for that office to answer, he turned to Mom. "We had some visitors' last night!"

The Sheriff arrived while we were eating breakfast. After having a cup of coffee, He, Dad and Merle went out to the holding pen with me tagging along.

When we arrived at the pen, Merle noticed something else was missing. "Dad, they got the cattle trailer too!" It had rained the evening before, and the story was there in the mud. The tracks showed that the thieves had taken the horse from the barn. They had then hitched the cattle trailer to a vehicle, and used the horse to drive the cows into the trailer. They had then loaded the horse in the trailer and driven off with the whole kit and caboodle! The noise they made had undoubtedly been covered by the thunder of the rainstorm.

As Dad stood looking down on the muddy tracks, the Sheriff said "Well, I need to get going if I'm going to find out who did this." Dad replied. "That's no problem. I know who did it!" He pointed to a tiny cowboy boot track in the mud. "Aleathia's nephew, Eddie is the only man I know that wears a boot that small! I've also a good hunch where he'll take them!"

My cousin, Eddie had been working for my dad as a hired man because good help was hard to find! Dad had fired him a couple of weeks before because he wouldn't show up for work on time. He was a pretty worthless individual. While Eddie was working on the farm, Dad had overheard him tell another cousin, "a man could make some easy money by stealing cattle, and taking them to Joplin Missouri to sell them!"

Eddie, like most thieves, was as stupid as he was dishonest. He followed his plan to the letter! However, by the time the Joplin livestock auction was notified, the cattle and horse had been sold, along with the trailer. Dad and the Sheriff had to go to Joplin to identify the property, and claim it.

This was not too difficult, as the cattle were branded, the trailer had a serial number, and the horse had identifying marks. The saddle had my dad's initials under the fender of one of the stirrups. The auction company had names and addresses of all the buyers.

My dad said that when he went to locate the horse, they found him at a rural school house near Neosho Missouri. The horse was at the school house because the man that bought him was the teacher at that school. He had bought the horse and saddle to ride to school because gasoline was rationed. Dad said that he felt sorry for the man, because, when he asked the Sheriff, in a plaintive voice, "What am I going to do?" the Sheriff replied, "I don't know, but you now know that you possess stolen property! I suggest that you return him to Joplin immediately to save yourself a lot of trouble!"

The horse, cattle, and trailer were returned to the Joplin auction where they had been purchased. In order to avoid possible criminal charges, the auction company offered to transport everything back home at no cost to Dad. They had a very good reason to do this!

At that time the area where we lived in Kansas was designated by law, a "Brand Area". This law required that all beef cattle more than a year old, in the area, and sold from the area, have a brand on them. Each farmer/rancher was required to register his brand with the state livestock commission. When these animals were sold, the seller was required to show his registration certificate as proof that he was the legal owner. This procedure was intended to prevent the sale of stolen cattle. Livestock auctions and stockyards were required to ask for the certificate. It was a felony to not do so! The livestock auction at Joplin had not done so!

When Eddie returned to Kansas, the Sheriff arrested him. After his arrest, in hopes of a lighter sentence, he implicated his brother, Sam, in the theft. It didn't work! The evidence in court showed that Sam was more of a patsy than an accomplice. Eddie had been arrested before. Sam hadn't been!

The judge wasn't stupid! He gave Eddie 3 years in the state prison. He gave Sam a choice of jail time or the military. Sam chose the military and fought on Iwo Jima! He received the purple heart and the silver star! After the war, he led an honorable life until his untimely death ten years later in a traffic accident.

I don't know what happened to Eddie after he got out of prison. I never saw him again, and never wanted to!

Chapter 17

Killers

It was a cold morning in early January. There was about six inches of snow on the ground. As Dad and I stood looking down at the gory mess, that had been six healthy sheep, I felt a terrible guilt! It was one of my chores, to lock the sheep safely in the sheep shed each evening. The previous evening, I had neglected to do so!

Next to a chicken, a sheep is the stupidest critter on the farm! It is also without any natural defense against any kind of attack. It has no horns, no sharp hooves, no sharp teeth, and it can't run fast. Sheep are totally dependent on the farmer for their welfare. Thus, every evening, they were herded into the sheep shed and locked in. The shed was a totally enclosed building that protected them from the weather, and any predators, that might come along during the night.

The marks and paw prints in the snow told the story! Examining the ground, Dad said "looks like there were seven of em! A pack that size has gotta be stopped quick!"

"How are we gonna do it?"

"Well, they were here, not more than a couple of hours ago. The carcasses are still warm and the blood hasn't frozen yet! I must have scared them off when I came out to milk!"

"Dad, I'm sorry! It's all my fault! I'll pay for them out of my own money !"

"Never mind that now! Let's hope the weather is clear tonight. There's a full moon. With this snow cover, they should be easy to see!"

"How do you know they'll be back tonight?"

"Because there's still some sheep alive! Once they start killing sheep, they'll keep comin' back as long as any sheep are left alive! If the sky's clear, it'll be almost as bright as day, outside! Can you hit any thing with that new coyote rifle you're so proud of?"

"If I can see em, I can kill em at 200 yards!"

"Well you're gonna get a chance to prove it! It's less than a hundred yards from the hay barn to the sheep shed. You've got a clear view from the barn loft. Now, let's get this mess cleaned up!"

The "coyote" rifle Dad was referring to was a Model 70 Winchester in .270 caliber. It had a 3X power scope sight. I had shot coyotes thru the head at 200 yards! Tonight, however, the target wasn't coyotes! It was something much worse!

It was Jim Outerbine's turn to drive to town to high school, that morning. Jim, Denny and I were in high school and we took turns driving to school. Elmo was a year behind us, and his dad wouldn't let him drive. He rode with us most of the time. On the way to school, I related what had happened. Jim got excited! He had a rifle identical to mine. "Hell, Bill, tomorrow's Saturday, so we don't have school! I'll come over tonight, and we'll give those varmints something they're not expectin'!"

That night the sheep were securely locked up. Jim came over, and Dad gave us our instructions.

"You boys dress warm. It's going to be cold up in that barn! Set your alarm clock. You don't need to go to the barn till about three o'clock. They won't come in until after that!"

I asked, "How do you know that?"

"They hit Elton's place last night before they came here!" Looking at me; "He had his sheep in the shed so they didn't do any damage! His dog woke him up, and he took a shot at em, but didn't hit any. I tracked em straight south from here, but lost their tracks on the road about 2 miles from here! They're runnin' a circuit!"

"How come we didn't hear Pinky, when they hit here?"

"Beats me!"

Jim and I got up at three o'clock, as instructed. We dressed, stepped outside and picked up our previously loaded rifles. We had left them on the porch so there would be no problem with our scopes fogging over in the cold. I looked at the thermometer as we left the rear porch. It read 10 degrees above zero! The night was so beautiful, it's hard to find the words to describe it! There were no man-made light sources to be seen. The full moon was directly overhead. The surface of the snow reflected the moonlight so brightly that I was able to read my watch! The stars glittered like diamonds on a canopy of black velvet! There was no wind. In the far distance, a coyote howled. The only other sound was the squeaking of the snow under our boots.

We reached the hay barn, climbed into the loft, and made ourselves as comfortable as possible. We were warmly dressed, so the cold wasn't bothering us. From where we sat, we had a clear view of the sheep shed through the barn loft door! We sat in silence, watching! The night dragged slowly by.

Suddenly, they are there! Or rather, their eyes are! They had approached in the shadow of a board fence, and are now in the shadow of the sheep shed! Deep in the shadow, we can't see their bodies. But, we can see the eyes which glow green with a malevolent fire, and hear the snarls as they try to get into the shed where the sheep are located! Up in the barn loft, we are above their normal line of sight. Neither can they smell us! They are on the near side of the sheep shed, about

75 yards away! I motion to Jim to take the left pair of eyes, while I take the right pair. I whisper, "on the count of three". Both rifles crack as one! Sound and flame splits the night apart! Two down! Animals out in the moonlight where we can see them! Again, flame from the rifle muzzles! Two more down! One runs around the hay barn, out of sight! The last two, by now, are going south running hard! The rifles crack again! Both stumble, then regain their feet and run on! Too far away and moving! We both miss! The echos of the rifles die away! Silence! I look at my watch. It is 4:45 AM.

We climbed down from the hay loft and went to the house. Dad had been up since four o'clock, but had stayed in the house so as to not spook the killers. He had stoked the wood stove and the kitchen was warm. He waited until we had removed our coats and caps, before he asked "Well?" We knew he was anxious, but we couldn't resist a little fun. As responsible boys, our dads treated us as young men, and not kids. I said "Have ya got any coffee made?"

"It's on the stove." (Gruffly)

"Four dead, two wounded, one escaped around the barn unhurt."

"How do ya know that two were wounded?"

"Cause, we rolled em, but they got up and kept runnin'!"

"Well, you and Jim stay here, and get warmed up. I'll take care of th' milkin'. Mom will be awake in a few minutes. After breakfast we'll take a look at your handiwork."

It was full daylight when, after breakfast, we went out to the sheep shed. The first two we had shot had almost no heads! A 150 grain soft nose bullet, traveling more than 3,000 feet per second, wreaks terrible damage on whatever it hits! The second two were fifty yards further away. The damage done to them is better left not described! We followed the remaining two by their tracks to the point where the bullets had hit them. From that point on, both were leaving blood on the snow. Dad suggested that we all get in the pickup and drive around to the next section road. If they crossed the road, we should spot the blood trails in the snow.

When we arrived on the section road one mile straight south of our place, we came upon the blood trails. However, only one crossed the road! The other led under a road culvert that was partially filled with snow. Dad kneeled down and looked in the culvert. "There's one in here, he's dead." Then, with a strange look on his face he said, "Jim, you better come take a look."

When Jim knelt down and peered into the culvert, his face turned white! In a strangled voice, he said "It's our dog, Rex!" That's what it was! It was the Outerbine dog!

The reason that my dad knew that the pack would be back, was because we knew that the killers were dogs, and not wild animals! My dad, having had experience with them years before, knew dog packs are creatures of habit! They will return at the first opportunity to the place where they last killed! Also, wild predators only kill in self defense, or for food! A pack of coyotes is capable of killing sheep. However, they will start to feed on the carcass as soon as the kill is made. The sheep we found had not been eaten on! They had been wantonly slaughtered and left. Only the interruption by Dad, had prevented the pack from killing more! Finally, the absolute proof were the tracks in the snow!

It is usually the case that packs of these dogs that roam at night are not strays! At dawn they separate, to return home and become the family pet! At night, however, they are far more vicious and dangerous than a pack of wolves.

Jim soon recovered from his shock and surprise! To a farmer, dogs had a useful purpose. Although little farm kids had emotional attachment to the dog of the moment, the adult men had very little. We loaded his dog in the back of the pick up and drove around the section to the next section road to see if we could pick up the blood trail again.

We almost missed it! The dog had come up a shallow draw and crossed under the road through a culvert directly in front of a neighbors house. We had been driving east. Jim was sitting on the right hand, or south side of the truck, with me in the center. As he looked out of his side of the truck, he saw a large dog that was limping! He yelled "There he is!" just as the dog went under the front porch of the house.

The house sat back some distance, on the south side of the east/west section line road. We had just gone past the driveway, so Dad backed up, and we went in. As we got out of the truck, the neighbor came out to greet us. The place belonged to Elton Ewell, but his hired man, Roy Barnes, lived in the house.

"Mornin' Roy"

"Mornin' Mr. Ross, mornin' Bill, mornin' Jim."

"Son, you and Jim go see if you find any blood. Roy, does that dog we just saw go under your porch belong to you?"

"Well I didn't see it go under. I was watchin' you fellers drive up. My dog's name is Bob. I'll call im'. Here Bob, com'ere Bob!"

The dog came out from under the porch. It was a beautiful black Labrador that went up to Roy to be petted. It was walking on three legs. The left front leg was missing about half way down it's length. Roy dropped to his knees beside his dog, who began to lick his face. "Bob, what happened to you? Mr. Ross, I'm glad you saw him! My wife loves this old dog. We've had em awhile!"

"I'm sorry Roy, but we didn't come to save em. We came to kill em!" (in a gentle voice)

"For Gawd's sake, why?"

"He's a sheep killer!"

"How do you know that?"

"He's missing a leg, because one of these boys shot it off at my place early this morning! We followed the blood trail here! Check his mouth!" Roy pried Bob's mouth open and upon reaching down between his teeth, pulled out wool fibers. This was the ultimate conviction of a sheep killer! Roy looked down at his dog. "Awww Bob, old boy!" Dad said "Bill, get your rifle"

As I started to the pickup, Roy said " I'll do it myself. Ain't there no other way out of it?"

Dad replied; "I'm afraid there ain't! You know that! But we'll do it! Bill, load old Bob in the pickup."

Jim and I loaded Bob in the back of the truck, and tied him to the bed with a rope around his neck. He sniffed at the carcass of the other dog and lay down beside it.

"I'm sorry Roy!"

"What hasta be, hasta be. Ya gotta do whatcha gotta do!"

When we got back to our place, with Bob in the back of the truck; Dad asked, "Where's Pinky?" Pinky was a Border Collie that we had gotten when he was a puppy. He was a very smart dog. Dad had taught him to herd the sheep and he was responsive to Dad's voice commands. He was getting on in years! He was now ten years old.

I answered Dad. "He's around someplace. Why do ya ask?"

"I want to see im."

"Okay! Here Pinky, Here Pinky!"

Pinky came running as he always did, when I called. Dad said; "Lemme look at him!" He opened Pinky's jaws, and pulled wool fibers from between his teeth!

"How did ya know?" I asked , when I got over my shock!

"I didn't know for sure, but he didn't bark night before last, when the sheep were killed. He didn't bark this morning when the pack returned. The dog that got away, ran around the barn. He didn't go south with the other two!"

A sheep killer cannot be cured! There is only one remedy available or allowed! Jim was given the distasteful job of applying the remedy to Pinky and Bob!

Chapter 18
Pie Suppers

"Which one is it?" Albert asked me.

"I've forgotten."

"How much would it take to refresh yer memory?"

"Two bucks should do it."

"You're a robber, but here's yer blood money! Now, which one is it?"

"It's the one with the large silver bell in the middle of the lid, and the little pink stars around it!"

"You're sure?"

"Yep"

Albert Ewell, and I were eyeing the many pretty boxes that sat on the several tables, awaiting the auction. Al, as he was called, wanted to know which box had been prepared by my sister! Because I was her younger brother, he figured that I knew which one it was! Al was "sweet on" my sister!

The occasion was a community pie supper. A couple of times a year, the school held one of these events to raise money for things not in the school budget. It worked as follows.

The date of the event would be announced in the local weekly newspaper. It was always held on a Saturday evening in the spring and fall seasons. It was always heavily attended. When the announcement was made, the women and girls of the community would start decorating boxes with crepe paper, foil, and other decorations. These boxes were about 16 inches square, and two to three inches deep. Inside the box were the women's culinary preparations. A typical box would always have two large pieces of homemade pie, and cake. In addition, they usually had a lot of other delectable goodies!

The boxes were placed on long tables and sold at auction! The buyer of the box, was required to eat with the woman or girl who made it!

The women were very secretive about the way the boxes were decorated. This was because none of the men and boys, who were bidding on the boxes, were supposed to know what female they were going to eat with! They only found out who she was, after they had bought the box! The only clues they had were that all unmarried girls box's had some kind of pink motif. The married women used a blue motif.

Well, in theory, this was the way it was supposed to work! However, a wife usually left her pie box laying somewhere at home, so that her husband could see it before the pie supper!

Woe unto the husband who failed to bid on his wife's pie box! My sister always let me see her efforts, with an admonition not to "tell anyone what it looks like." This was pure baloney of course! We both understood that she wanted me to tell Al Ewell!

There were a couple of unwritten rules of thumb about a pie supper. With pink boxes, it was "The prettier the box, the uglier the girl!" With blue boxes, it was "The prettier the box, the worse the food!" My mom was known as an excellent cook, so she always made her pie box pretty; operating on the theory that Dad could buy it fairly cheap! My sister did the same, thinking that only Al would know it was her pie box. These were very good theories, but they didn't work, for a very simple reason!

ME!

It was springtime, and the weather was warm. Most of the men were standing around outside the building, engaged in conversation, waiting for the auction to begin. It was getting dark, and the yard lights were on. After collecting my two dollars from Al, I went outside. I had only been outside a couple of minutes, when a fellow strolled up beside me. It was John Lynn, one of Al's buddies. Everyone called him J.L. (Al and his buddies were about four years older than me.) "What's Sue's pie box look like?"

"It'll cost ya!"

"How much?"

"Fifty cents."

J. L. gave me two quarters, and received the same information, I had given Al. The reason that I had charged him less, was because I knew he only wanted to run the price up on Al! He wouldn't have paid as much extortion money as Al had.

In the next half hour, I made another $2.50, at fifty cents a pop. Two more of Al's buddies bribed me, and three of Dad's neighbors got information about Mom's pie box!

When we got home that night, Dad said to Mom "You women are goin' to have to start usin' plain boxes! Ole Al and me had to pay twice what any other box sold for!"

Chapter 19
Bedtime

Pooof, thud, thud, thud, then, 2 seconds of silence! **WHAM!** Ole Merle hit the floor like a ton of bricks! The entire room shook! I sat up in my bed and yelled "What happened?" The only response from Merle was a groan and a couple of cuss words! Dad came running up the stairs with a flashlight. Mom was right behind him! The flashlight beam revealed Merle sitting on the floor looking dazed!

It was the summer of my ninth year, just before Merle enlisted in the air force. Since we didn't yet have electricity, Mom hurried to the table beside my bed and lit a lamp. The lamp revealed that Merle's bed was not in it's regular place in the room.

Our house was a large two story affair. It had 3 bedrooms upstairs. There was my sister's bedroom, and a guest bedroom. Merle and I slept in the 3rd bedroom. This was the largest room of the three. The first floor consisted of a large kitchen, dining room, living room, parlor, and my parent's bedroom. The ceilings on the first floor were nine feet high.

I will try to describe the upstairs floor plan to the reader. The stairs coming up were straight and long. At the top on the newel post there was a kerosene lamp. The last person to go to bed was supposed to blow out the lamp and make their way down the hallway to bed. Since Merle was generally the last one to go to bed, this was his task. The bedroom that Merle and I slept in was about 15 feet straight down the hall from the newel post. Our doorway was at the end of the hall.

Merle and I each slept in 3/4 size beds. Merle's bed was straight in from the door about eight feet, and turned at a right angle to the opening. My bed was at the other end of the room. Both beds were mounted on casters, so that they could be moved for cleaning.

That afternoon, Mom had swept the bedroom floor. She had moved Merle's bed aside while she was cleaning.

Now, my brother had a couple of phobias that created problems for him. One was, that at 19, he was afraid of the dark! So his usual practice was to blow out the newel post light, run the length of the hall, launch himself through our door, and sail through the air to his bed! While in the air, he would turn himself in such a way that he lit in his bed on his back! If I wasn't asleep, I could always hear him. Tonight had been the same. *EXCEPT, the bed wasn't there!*

When she saw Merle on the floor, Mom said "Oh dear, I guess I forgot to move the bed back in place after I cleaned the floor!" I made no comment! Dad was suspicious. "Billboy, do you know anything about this?"

"Well, he jumped across the room like he always does."

"Why do you do that?" (to Merle)

"unintelligible mumble."

"Are you hurt?"

"mumble."

"Answer me!"

"I don't reckon I am."

"Well, get up and get in bed! You've got a clean up job in the morning!"

"Why"

"Because, you knocked about 10 square feet of plaster off the living room ceiling!"

There are times when silence is golden! So I didn't tell anyone that Mom hadn't forgotten to put Merle's bed back in place. Neither did I tell them that I had again moved it! Sometimes, little brothers are a pain in places other than the neck!

Chapter 20
Ice Skating

"I'm gonna give er a try" Elmo said, looking down at his toboggan.

I said, "I don't think that's a good idea Crawdad!"

"I'm gonna try er anyhow!"

Sue asked "Why do you guys call him Crawdad?" as she watched Elmo trudge up the hill.

"It's a long story and you wouldn't like it anyway!"

Sue and I were standing in a group of about nine or ten people on the ice of Ewell's pond. It was a Friday night, about nine o'clock in mid February. Earlier in the week the good ole boys had decided to have a hay ride and ice skating party.

It was about 20 degrees above zero, and the farm ponds were frozen deep enough to support a skater's weight. We planned to take a tractor and hay trailer and ride the 2 miles to Ewell's pond. This was the same pond in which Elmo had earned his nickname.

The month of February in Kansas was usually bad weather with blowing, drifting snow. The last storm had been unusual. There had been no wind and the snow had fallen straight down to a depth of about six inches.

Everything had gone as planned, except that when Sue had found out that we were planning to invite some neighborhood girls, she had invited herself to come along! She told my folks that she was going along to "protect the girls from that pack of ignorant boys!" Actually, she had found out that Al Ewell was going!

These parties were always a lot of fun! Everyone would dress warmly and hop on the loose hay on the trailer. We would slowly meander down the road to the pond! Upon arriving at the pond, we would light a giant fire from wood that we had hauled there earlier in the week. As the evening wore on, couples would skate for awhile and return to the fire to roast marshmallows and drink hot chocolate.

Everyone that is, except Elmo! Elmo was always trying to be a daredevil and show off for the girls! He didn't understand, although he had been told, that the girls didn't care for those kind of antics!

Well, Elmo paid no attention to what I had said! He climbed up the hill to the top and yelled "watch me, here I come!" With that he jumped on his toboggan and started down toward the pond like a bat outta of hell!

Now, as I described in another chapter, this pond was fairly deep except at one end! The pond was spring fed. This little spring ran year round thru warm and freezing weather. It fed into the shallow end of the pond. The hill that Elmo was careening down ended in a 3 foot drop off directly into this shallow water.

Elmo had a couple of problems! First, his toboggan wasn't really a toboggan! It was a piece of galvanized roofing metal about two feet wide, and four feet long. He had drilled a couple of holes in one end and attached a piece of rope to hold on to. The metal didn't curve up on the end like a regular toboggan! It was flat, with a sharp edge! His second problem was a trick of nature. At the bottom of the hill, about six feet in front of the drop off there was a small stump! It was only about 6 inches tall, but that was enough!

When ole Elmo came whizzing down the hill, several things happened! The front end of his toboggan hit the stump! The toboggan stopped! Elmo didn't! He did a complete flip while he flew about fifteen feet through the air! He landed on his bottom on the ice at the shallow end of the pond! And went right on through it!

The ice over the shallow running water wasn't nearly as thick as the rest of the ice! Elmo wound up sitting on the muddy bottom in about eight inches of water and two inches of ice!

This put an end to the skating party. As soon as we got Elmo home, we wrapped him in blankets and put him in front of the stove to thaw out. After his teeth stopped chattering, he looked at Jim and I. In a relieved voice, He said Hooboy!

"I'm sure glad those danged crawdads are hibernatin' this time of year!"

Chapter 21

Beauty

As I knelt beside her, Beauty rubbed her nose against the palm of my hand, knowing that I had a carrot hidden on me somewhere. I produced the carrot and scratched between her ears as she contentedly chewed it and looked at me with big brown trusting eyes.

Beauty was a beautiful black quarter horse mare, with a white star in the middle of her forehead. Dad had purchased her as a yearling. When he brought her home, he said to me, "This little mare is your's. She's just halter broke, so you will have to train her yourself! What are you going to name her?"

I was ten years old, and just finished reading a book about a mare who was colored black. I instantly said "Black Beauty" after the horse in the book. So it was. Everyone left off the "Black" and called her Beauty.

As time passed, I did train her. By the time she was a four year old, I had trained her to be a cattle horse. Meanwhile, I taught myself how to handle a lariat. She was a quick study, and extremely quick on her feet! She became a wonderful cutting horse! I could drop the reins on the saddle horn and guide her with the pressure of my legs!

One time, at a small local rodeo, a friend and I were both entered in the calf roping contest. He had a nice little pinto that I knew was not as quick as Beauty. In a roping contest, speed is everything! The roper backs his horse into an area known as a chute, a few feet behind a rope barrier. The calf was turned loose and given a head start. When the calf was about 25 feet out, the barrier was dropped! When the barrier dropped, a timer started. The object was to lasso the calf, get off the horse, and tie 3 of the calf's legs together in the least amount of time! Beauty knew the game! She had done it many times before!

She knew what was coming when I put the pigging string between my teeth, draped the loop of the lariat over my right shoulder, and backed her in behind the barrier.

Some rider's horses were trained to not move until the reins went slack. Not Beauty! When I backed her into the chute, I looped the reins loosely around the saddle horn and got a firm grip on the horn with my left hand! I felt her hindquarters slightly squat down as she gathered her rear legs beneath her. I nodded to the barrier man that I was ready. When I did this, three things happened almost simultaneously. The calf shot into the arena at a dead run! The barrier dropped!

Beauty cleared 10 feet on the first jump, and was at a dead run at the end of the third stride! Within 100 feet, she would be directly along the side of the calf. At that point, all I had to do was drop the loop over the calf's head and let the rope run out. When the noose went on the calf, she would already be sliding to a stop with her rear legs under her to take the shock of the calf hitting the end of the rope!

Well, my friend approached me and told me he had a problem. "Bill, my horse has come up lame."

"Well ya can use Beauty."

"That's great, I sure appreciate it!"

"There's just a couple a things."

"What are they?"

"Ya gotta take your spurs off! She ain't used ta spurs!"

"No problem! What else?"

"When you're in th' chute, loop the reins on the saddle horn. and hang onto th' horn when the barrier drops!"

He just grinned at me!

A few minutes later, he wasn't grinning. He was picking himself up out of the dirt, while the horse stood about a hundred feet away, looking back at him as if to say "What're ya doin' back there?" He hadn't followed my advice about hanging on to the saddle horn. Beauty ran out from under him on the first jump!

Now, it was many years later! I was a grown man and no longer lived on the farm, and she hadn't been ridden in a number of years. Dad had called me and said "Son, you better come over home. Beauty's down out in the pasture."

When I stood up, she tried to rise! She couldn't make it! My voice cracked as my eyes blurred! Finally I managed to say in a gentle voice, "It'll be okay girl." She looked up at me with those trusting eyes, as I looked down at the white star in her forehead over the sights of the rifle ***********!

About the Author

Bill Ross is a retired real estate broker. He lives with his wife of 44 years in the beautiful Ozarks of southern Missouri. His childhood on a farm in Kansas has always been treasured memories to Bill. It seemed a shame to him that the era of those "good ole farm boys" should slip quietly into the past. He began writing those memories as a legacy for his family, then discovered how interested others were in his stories. No one is more surprised than Bill that this book has developed. "I sure never thought of myself as a writer," he says. "I just know that you can remove a boy from the farm, but you can never remove the farm from the boy!"